Breaking the Chains

With Spiritual Healing

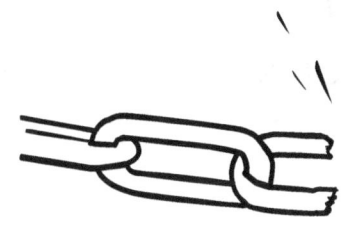 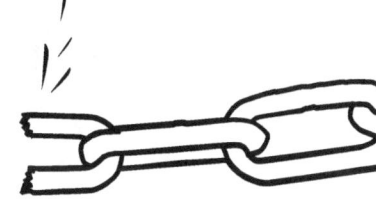

Consuelo Cardenas

Published by Dolphin Star

DolpHin Star

Copyright © 2019 by Consuelo Cardenas.
All rights reserved.

This book or any portion thereof may not be reproduced or used in any manner whatsoever without the express written permission of the publisher except for the use of brief quotations in a book review.

Printed in the United States of America.

First Printing, 2019

ISBN 978-0-9827408-4-2

Consuelo Cardenas

Changed

You went away
And left me here.
You tore my heart
Like every year.
When you were gone,
I met someone
Who gave me love
Like no other one.
His name is Jesus.
As you can see,
He changed my life
And set me free.
So if you want a life with me.
Let God change you
And be set free.

Help Me

Lord.
Help me to love
Like you love me.
Help me to see
The way you see me.
Help me to hear
The way you hear me.
Help me to talk
The way you talk to me.
Help me to walk
The way you walk with me.
Help me to laugh,
The way you laugh with me.
Help me to cry,
The way you cry with me.
Help me to encourage,
The way you encourage me.
Help me to carry my weight,
Like you carried the cross.
Help me to die to my sin,
That I may be made whole again.

Consuelo Cardenas

You're Not Alone

He had a plan.
Right from the start.
For you and me,
He gave His heart.
The trials that came
Were very harsh.
But he made it through
For me and for you.
The trials we have
Cannot compare
To what our Lord
Was going through.
So when in pain,
Remember this:
You're not alone.
Our pain is His.

Set Free

There will come a day
When you will see
How Jesus came
And set me free.
He came through trials
That came my way.
I had no knowledge
What was coming my way.
I trusted the world,
As you can see,
Know I'm paying the price.
I was too blind to see.
But Jesus came in
And He set me free.
Know I'm serving the Lord.
Because He cares for me.

Consuelo Cardenas

Room for Change

A room can be
A place to sleep.
A room can be
A place to weep.
A room can be
A place to kneel.
A place where
You are real.
A room can be
A mountain top.
Where change will come
When you meet God.

Orphan

You say that
You're an orphan.
You say nobody cares.
You say that you
Were left alone.
Your parents were just
Not there.
But just remember, child.
It's not that they didn't care.
How can they stay around,
When they were never there?
In this world,
We're all orphans.
But our parents are still there.
But how can they be parents
If God does not reside there.
Oh no, you're not an orphan.
Your Father lives in you.
He said He'll never leave you.
You see He's my Father too.

Consuelo Cardenas

A Change within

Remember the things that you can see.
Remember the sounds that you can hear.
Remember each day that brings us near.
To each family member that we love so dear.
Remember the joy when we once laughed.
Remember the time that we sat and chat.
Remember the things that we once feared.
Remember the hurts that brought us to tears.
Remember the church that brought us cheer.
Remember the God who broke our fear.
Remember the day we all received
The Holy Spirit and laughed with tears.
Remember the change that came within.
Remember again, you're not the same.
Remember that things that you once had seen.
You'll never see them the same again.

Yes You Can

You say you can't do it.
But God says you can.
You say you're not smart enough.
But God says you're enough.
You say you're a failure,
God says don't give up.
You say no one loves you,
Yet Jesus died on the cross.
You say you'll try later.
God says do it now.
Tomorrow's not promised.
Step into now.

Consuelo Cardenas

I Know I Can

I know I can do it.
He said I can.
He's our creator of everything.
He's the great I Am.
I know I can do it.
He said I can.
Just put my hand to it.
And He'll guide your hand.
I know I can do it.
He said I can.
He'll guide my life through it.
And I know I can.

Rocks and Pebbles

Getting old together
Is is a journey in itself.
There are rocks and pebbles everywhere.
You're already in despair.
But God keeps saying, "Focus,
The road will soon be clean.
Those big rocks that are blocking you
Will soon disappear.
Those big rocks that you're seeing.
Might look very big to you.
But to me its just a pebble,
That I can blow away from you."

Consuelo Cardenas

A New Heart

As God is my witness
I want you to know
How God changed my heart
And he set my soul free.
It starts with our heart
God told me, you see.
So give me the old heart
And you will have me.
We've gone through the journey
As blind as can be.
Trying to fix things
That were inside of me.
The harder I tried.
The worse it would be.
I couldn't get things to happen
The way I wanted them to be.
So I gave God my heart
And I know I can see
That all I ever needed
Was a heart transplant
In me.

Cross Streets

They come
And they go
On His cross roads of life.
Carrying their backpacks
As they leave everything behind.
They laugh
And they cry
And they dance
Their way through.
These streets of a neighborhood
Where the violence is so cruel.
They've all heard of Jesus.
And some know His word.
But surrender to addiction,
Instead of His hope.
They come and they go.
On these cross streets of life.
Not knowing that the cross streets
Are a symbol of life.

Consuelo Cardenas

The More of God

The more of God
Is always here.
We tend to miss it
Because of fear.
We want to see
The things we want
But only God knows where to start.
God brings to pass
The things we fear
So He can show us
And make it clear
That if we wait
And call on God
He'll bring to pass
The peace we lost.

Blowing Trumpets

When angels are around us
They blow their trumpets loud
So we can hear them calling
The Lord is in our lives.
We turn to other people
For answers we can't hear
When all the time the trumpets
Are blowing loud and clear.

Consuelo Cardenas

A Chance

The trees dry up
So does the grass.
Our bodies dry up
Just like that grass.
It's plain to see
We are not free.
Will fade away
As fast as can be.
So water yourself
So family can see
That there is a chance
For you to be free.

A Life Changed

God is my Savior.
God is my Lord.
God is who saved me.
As I walked in the door,
I raised up my hands.
And worshiped the Lord
Not knowing my life,
Had just made a turn.

Consuelo Cardenas

In the Word

You cry.
You scream.
You laugh.
In Between.
You hurt.
You say,
"I'm sorry
I did it again."
But all in all,
I love you, my dear.
You'll forget it tomorrow.
It's a new year.
The hurt and the pain
Will all go away.
Believe me, my angel,
It's all been my way.
Just give it to God
And trust in the Lord.
He'll make you feel better.
It's all in His Word.

Four Corners

Four corners
They call it.
Four corners
It's there.
Four corners
You're in it.
It's called a jail.
Four corners
You call it.
Four corners
It's there.
It's also you're bedroom
And you spend all your time there.
Four corners
You call it.
Four corners
It's there.
It's Jesus standing
In the doorway.
Showing you four corners.
The four corners
On which he died
Of love for you.

Consuelo Cardenas

Water the Roots

We tend to hang on
To the things that have gone dry.
We blame everybody
Our mind is so blind.
We water the plants
We water the yard.
What we should be watering
Is the sin in our heart.
Don't let your heart go dry.
As you can see
You're the root
Of your family.
And it will start
With thee.

Step Out

Fear can grip you
If you let your guard down.
It will steal everything
That you have around.
It will steal your Joy.
It will steal your peace.
It will steal your identity.
You'll no longer exist.
The person you were.
Is no where to be found.
You're hiding in darkness.
You're life has gone down.
So set yourself out,
And let the light shine.
God has been waiting
To bring the light down.

Consuelo Cardenas

God's Presence

Learn to forgive
And you will see
The trouble you carry
Will no longer be.
Peace you have asked,
Peace you will get.
Trust in the Lord
And He will give.
Learn to forgive
And you will see.
That family together
Is the way is should be.
Learn to forgive
And you will feel
God's presence inside you;
That's how God likes to heal.

Angel on Wheels

You sit on a wheelchair
All through the day,
Doing God's work
Until the end of the day.
We should learn from you
As we go through the day
Complaining and crying
About everything that comes our way.
If there is a lesson
That should be learned
It's not to give up
No matter what.
You're a blessing to me
Because God showed me
That we're all in a wheelchair
Spiritually.

Consuelo Cardenas

Power of Love

The power of love
Is all in you're heart.
Open the door
Don't let it stay shut.
Let love shine in.
It's never too late.
Jesus is watching;
His power is great.
The power of love
We have it within.
Don't make the mistake
Of ignoring it again.

One Sheep

You say you love Him.
But you don't care.
The hurt you carry
You cannot bare.
You hurt so much
You want to leave.
But the love you carry
Is also deep.
Jesus carried the cross
For you and me.
His love for us
Was also deep.
So if you're hurting
And you want to leave
Remember when Jesus
Went to look for one sheep.
He left all
Just to get one.
What are you putting
In front of that one?

Consuelo Cardenas

Fighting for Life

When cancer comes
And disrupts your life
Darkness sets in
With no where to hide.
You cry and you cry
And to no avail.
The fear is so deep
You just don't care.
But hope is near.
So dry your eyes.
Get up and fight.
In you, He lives.

Prepare to Fight

When I lie in my bed
Away in my thoughts,
I look at my husband
Who is right by my side.
Remember how
We came through these years
Like a merry go round.
There was no finish here.
We're laughed and we've cried,
My husband and I.
But the laughing has stopped.
God's prepared me to fight.
It's no laughing matter
When Satan's involved.
He'll tear up your marriage
If you're not prayed up.
So get on your knees,
If possible, two.
God says when two come together.
He is there with you.

Consuelo Cardenas

Don't give up

Don't give up.
It's a new day.
Tomorrow's not promised,
So live for today.
God gave you to us
So that we could see
That you're more than a brother,
You're our only brother you see.
So put on your smile.
And listen to me;
The pain that you carry
Is also in me.
But just knowing Jesus
Can and will
Set you free.
You say how do I know this?
Because it happened to me.

Jesus Keeper

You wake in the morning
And what do you do?
You feel all the pains
That are coming on you.
You lay there and think
Why you're feeling this way
When all you had to do
Was get up and pray.
So as you wake up each day
Remember who's there.
It's you're brother, Jesus.
He's always been there.
Those things you are feeling
Will soon fade away.
The flesh is so used
To getting its way.
Remember we're here
For one thing you see;
It's to bring souls to Jesus,
So they can be set free.

Consuelo Cardenas

Covered Sin

A change will come;
A day in our lives.
We'll see our sin
As the stars in the sky.
Yes many there will be.
As you can see.
They will be erased
From your life.
As you will see.
Every scar that you had,
Will no longer be.
Because Jesus covers all
With His Love
That he gives
Unconditionally.

God's Gift

God gave you eyes
So you could see.
God give you ears
So you could hear.
He gave you lips
So you could speak
The word of God
That is so near.
He gave you hands
So you could touch
And lay a hand
On someone lost.
He gave you knees
So you could kneel
And pray for someone who needs to heal.
He gave you feet
So you could walk
And tell that lost someone,
God's down the block.

Consuelo Cardenas

Your Guide

Forgiving is important.
You want to make it through.
The journey that your taking
Will be hard and than a few.
So if you want to make it
Than you need to follow through.
Let Jesus come and guide you.
His steps will guide you through.

Put on the Armor

Watch your life wisely
As you can see.
There's someone in darkness
Waiting for thee.
He sit and waits
And laughs at our ways.
He sits there patiently
Laughing all day.
Put God in your life
And you will see
The armor of God
Coming to thee.

Consuelo Cardenas

Fishing for Souls

Fish we catch,
Fish we eat.
Fish is good we say to eat.
Souls we bring into the Lord
To feed the world
And know the Lord.
Fishing is fun
Don't get me wrong.
But fishing for souls
Is what God wants.

Love

Love is good.
Love is great.
Live your life
With love inside it.
Love is real.
Love can heal.
God brings love
To those who kneel.

Consuelo Cardenas

God's Creation

When God created angels
He had you in mind.
He knew you existed
Before our time.
In all the world's trouble
And all the world's pain,
He knew His creation
Was not in vain.
We're here for a reason
And God knows why;
If its only to love you
As the seasons arrive.

Non-Stop Prayer

Pray by day.
Pray by night.
Don't let your guard down;
Satan is roaming around.
He'll steal your joy
He'll steal your love.
He'll steal your peace
He's always around.
And where ever you are,
God's always there with you,
He's got your back.
So get in prayer.

Consuelo Cardenas

To Day

Outside my window
A new day I see,
And only God can determine
What kind of day it will be.
It can be busy and sunny,
Laughing all day.
Or blowing ice cold,
Unhappy and gray.
My own state of mind
Is the determining key.
For I am only a person
I let myself to be.
I can be thoughtful
With what I can give,
Or I can be selfish
And just think of myself.
I can enjoy what I do.
And make it seem fun.
Or gripe and complain
And make it hard on someone.
I can be patient
With those who don't understand.
Or belittle and hurt them
As much as I can.
But I have faith in myself.
Believe me when I say,
"I'll personally make
The best of each day."

A Special Gift

He's here today
But gone tomorrow.
He lost many years
Just worrying
About tomorrow.
Camping and holidays too,
He lost out on spending;
Special birthdays
With you.
But its never too late
To say I love you.
Tomorrow's not promised.
Make it a special
Present from you.

Consuelo Cardenas

The Crown of Hope

We have a crown
That we all wear.
A crown of hope
We need to share.
The crown of thorns
That Jesus wore
Reminds us of
The sin we store.
The crown of hope
He gave to me,
Removed the thorns
I had in me.
The crown of hope
He gave to me.
He saved my life
And set me free.

Raise your Hand

Today it hurts.
Today I sleep.
Today I felt
The thing I need.
Today I read,
Today I wrote.
Today I captured
All of the hurt.
Today He spoke
Through all my pain
And laid the cross
Right in my hand.
He told me, "Raise
Your hand up high,
And praise the Lord.
You will be fine."

Consuelo Cardenas

God's Mercy

Today's struggles
Are only today's.
Don't count on tomorrow;
Its another day.
What you feel today
Has passed and gone through.
Thank God for His mercy;
God's guiding you.

Moving On

A year has passed
Since that dreadful day
We lost our house
On a winter day.
We couldn't see
The mistakes we did.
We were too proud
To admit our fault.
But then one day
We turned around
Just to see
That is was gone.
But it's okay
Because you see
God removed the blinds from me
That I would see
That what we had
Really never belonged to me.
God said "One day,
You'll walk alone
Taking nothing
To the throne."
Where you live
It's plain to see.
God's using you
To set people free.

Consuelo Cardenas

Let Go

You say you're hurting.
You say you're sad.
You say everybody
Has turned their backs.
But it's okay.
My friend, you see,
Jesus will never
Turn His back on thee.
He takes my hand
And walks with me.
Taking me to a land
Of promises He gave to me.
I've entered this place
He gave to me.
It's a place of peace
And harmony.
The hurt and sadness
That I once had
Has turned into love
That I never had.
So let go, my friend,
And you will see
That peace that will carry you
Through the valley of harmony.

Left Behind

You walked this world
Filling empty inside
Wishing things would have turned out right.
But all you felt
Was deep despair,
Hoping somebody
Would be there.
You left your home
With sadness inside,
Trying to forget
What you left behind.
But then one day,
God spoke to you
And said, "My Son,
Just come to me.
The things you said you left behind
Were never yours.
They were mine.
I put you here
For just one thing;
To show the world
How I come in.
I came through you
As you will see.
I will use you,
To set people free."

Consuelo Cardenas

We're Not Alone

When times get hard
And your mind gets weary,
Reflect on God;
He's by your side already.
Ask Him for strength
That will get you through.
The Holy Spirit
Will guide you.
We're not alone,
As you can see.
Someone out there
Is praying for you.

Fight or Flight

You're getting angry
And you know not why.
You snap at your loved one
And say good-bye.
The love that you carry
Is buried inside.
Too deep inside you
It's no where in sight.
You wake up and wonder
What happened last night.
The one that you married
Is nowhere to be found.
The Devil's a liar.
He's ready to fight.
Don't let him take over
You're marriage tonight.
If you will remember
When Jesus told you,
"You are my child,
And I'm fighting for you."

Consuelo Cardenas

Love Them Anyway

You say you got hurt
Many times in your life
That all you can do
Is repeat what they do.
Repeating yourself
Is not what to do.
It's doing what Jesus
Has told you to do.
He wants you to love
Unconditionally.
And show them the way
God wants them to be.
By hurting yourself
It's hurting God too.
Because you see
Jesus lives in you too.
Its hard to love someone
Who has hurt you.
But than they don't know Jesus
As well as you do.

Joy

When you have Jesus
In your heart,
No if's or cant's
Will enter your mind.
You'll walk with joy
In your heart
And love everybody.
No matter what
The Lord is good
To everyone.
So stay plugged in
And you will see
How God will move
In you joyfully.

Consuelo Cardenas

Glued Together

You've come together
As husband and wife
You bought a home.
God's made it right.
You're holding jobs
And that is good.
Now pray to God
To glue it good.

Rooted Out

Don't let the fear
Grab your life.
It sucks you in
And drains you out.
It'll make your life
Impossible to live.
It will make you scared stiff.
The only way
To wipe it off
Is in God's word.
He'll get you out.
The word is strong.
It penetrates deep.
It'll cut the root
And let you sleep.

Consuelo Cardenas

Never Alone

The time is coming
And you will see
That being alone
Will set you free.
Time alone
Is what we need.
We talk to God
Patiently.
He hears our prayers
Day and night.
We're never alone
He's always there.
Enjoy your time
Alone with God.
He'll speak to you
Through lonely nights.

Listen

People will come
To tell you their problems.
Don't run away.
It will help you
With your own problems.
Listen and learn
What they're saying to you.
God might be speaking
Through that other person
To you.
Listen and listen
And listen some more.
You might be saving a life,
So just listen and learn.

Consuelo Cardenas

The Right Route

I wish I could,
I wish I would.
I wish my mind
Took a delightful route.
The mind is good
If your thoughts are good.
It's also bad
If your thoughts are bad.
So pray to God
And let Him know
He's ready to take
Full control.

God's Grace

You want to be lost
In this world, you say.
You hide from the people
Who can show you the way.
The enemy lies,
To you every day.
And you grabs everything
He throws your way.
You'll lose family,
If you don't let go.
The devil is laughing
At you every day.
Just watching and waiting
For you to say,
"I'm tired of living,
So take me away."
But you see, my friend,
It doesn't have to be.
Give God a chance
To show you His grace,
And to show the Devil
That you've won the race.

Consuelo Cardenas

The Will

Roses are Red
Violets are Blue.
I wish I could pray
The hurt off of you.
You're God's creation,
And He called you a rose.
He'll love you forever.
Just believe in him, Rose.
I know you are hurting,
Deep down inside.
It feels like a never ending fight.
But believe and pray,
And all will be well,
Because I also met Jesus
Down at the well.

You Had it All

I have ears
But I can't hear.
I have eyes
But I can't see.
I have lips,
But I can't speak.
I have a heart
But I don't feel.
I have a mind,
But I don't think.
I have feet
But I wont walk.
I had Jesus,
But He said to me,
"You had it all,
But you traded me..."

Consuelo Cardenas

Long Nights

Sometimes we walk
Though life alone
Not knowing where
Our life will go.
The nights seem long
As we go through,
When we start walking
Our life with you.
But as we pray,
And seek the Lord,
The nights we dread
Will be no more.
So seek the Lord
With all your heart,
And know that Jesus
Is there tonight.

A New Relationship

You left your hometown
To get a new start.
You thought the grass
Was greener on the other side.
But you found out it wasn't.
Temptation is here.
Temptation is there.
The Devil is also everywhere.
He'll whisper to you,
"Have a drink or two.
Go look for a party,
You'll be all right.
Would I lie to you?"
You see tomorrow's not promised.
And we're all going home.
But why listen to the Devil?
You see he's out to get you.
He's got many trophies
And he also wants you.
Start a relationship with Jesus.
He's the only father for you.

Consuelo Cardenas

Don't Doubt

The day will come
And you'll see the light
Of all the things
That were not right.
You will reflect
What you did wrong.
And go through a test
Of fear and doubt.
But as you focus
On the Lord,
He'll bring you out.
There is no doubt.
Remember this
And remember it well:
Jesus never leaves us,
He's always there.

Gift of Love

Christmas is coming
And its time to give cheer.
And celebrate Jesus;
He's the reason we're here.
He gave us a gift
Of cheer and of joy
And said not to worry,
Just call it all joy.
So celebrate Christmas
And remember that day
His greatest gift ever
Is the love that He gave.

Consuelo Cardenas

Stay Focused

Through our life
We follow men
Just to find out
We had a dead end.
Our life will go on,
With no end in sight.
And get hurt on the way
Because we went the wrong way.
So get your eyes off
What the world wants to give.
Satan shows you the best of it
And than reels you in.
So focus on Jesus
And give praises to Him.
And you're life will be better.
Because you let Him in.

Setting the Fire

We look here,
We look there.
We're looking for something
That will make our life fair.
But we're living
In a make believe world
When we should be reaching
All the lost souls.
The joy that I want
Is deep down inside.
Its the Holy Spirit
Setting the fire inside.
Oh what joy you can have
If you just don't give up.
Jesus is waiting,
So let your fire
Flare up.

Consuelo Cardenas

My Friend

When nights are lonely.
And your pain is deep
Just turn to God
Because God doesn't sleep.
He'll wake you up
And let you know.
It is all right
For you to let go.
I looked around
And who was there?
It was a friend
Who really cared.
He took me in,
And cared for me.
And told me that
I was His friend.
I thank the Lord
For helping me.
You see, my friend,
He's living in me.

Thank God

We complain about our future
We complain about our past.
We complain about where we live
And don't thank God
For where were are.
We complain about our children.
We complain about our needs.
We complain about our illness
When Jesus already took care of it.
We complain about our husbands.
We complain about our wives.
We forget who gave it all to us.
It was our Lord, Jesus Christ.

Consuelo Cardenas

A Place of Comfort

A mother is someone special.
A mother is someone sweet.
She will hug you
When you're going through it
And feed you
When you want to eat.
She'll open the door
And let you in.
And comfort you
Till that smiles comes in.
A mother should be treasured
And loved and hugged the same.
Because God didn't make her
A heart of stone.
He form it with His hands.

Homeward Bound

Life is like the wind
Is passes very fast.
You'll feel it for a moment.
You won't know when it passed.
You'll put things off till tomorrow,
But tomorrow comes too fast.
Before we even know it,
Now you're aging really fast.
Don't put off till tomorrow
What you can do today.
You see you're home
Is in the book of life
And you may be on you're way.

Consuelo Cardenas

Give it Your All

Love is good.
Love is not blind.
Love will come soon.
Just give it some time.
Love also heals
Where you need it the most.
It doesn't come easy;
You got to give it your all.
So get on your knees
And pray to the Lord.
Ask Him for love
And see the healing flow.

Faithful Savior

The Lord is so faithful
He's always on time.
He brought us a Savior
To come heal the blind.
He'll open our eyes.
So we can see.
That even in darkness
We will be set free.

Consuelo Cardenas

Tears of Love

The tears I shed
Are tears of love.
God shed His tears
It was all love.
He shed His tears
For you and for me.
He loves us all unconditionally.
So as you shed
You're tears each day.
Shed them for your children.
And love them more each day.

Breaking the Chains with Spiritual Healing

Devil in Disguise

He comes all dressed up
In his camouflaged suit.
He comes and he goes
Speaking the word.
He says, "I'm an angel,"
He says, "Please hear my word."
He wants you to follow
That he'll make it right.
He knows you're addicted
And says it will be all right.
He'll say, "Take a drink.
Just don't make it two.
You know you're addicted
But its really up to you.
I'll come back tomorrow
And check on you.
Enjoy that one beer."
Who's fooling who?

Consuelo Cardenas

Bring on Laughter

Laughter is good
For the mind.
Laughter is good
For the soul.
Laughing is good
For the broken.
It can mend
The heart and soul.
Laughs heal the body
It makes you want to dance.
It makes you jump up and down
With no more pain at last.
Laughing is the medicine
We should be looking for.
It covers all the misery
That the devil has brought forth.

The Light Within

Wasted days,
Wasted nights
Is how I feel.
There is no light.
I need someone
To bring me out.
This wasted time
Is a losing bout.
I need to see
The light within,
And know that God
Will reel me in.

Consuelo Cardenas

God's Beauty

We go through the mountains
When we go to fish.
To mountains so high
They cannot be reached.
But the deeper we go,
Deeper inside
We're surrounded by beauty
It's all in our sight.
I look at the mountains
And trees and the rocks.
And see God's creation
And have peace in my life.
All things are well-rooted
As you can see.
That's just like Jesus
Wants us to be.

Troubled Heart

There is a closeness
Of two people in love.
They're inseparable
Where ever they are.
They share all their thoughts
And share them with love.
There's nothing between them,
Just love in their heart.
They never have time
To find errors in them.
Because God made no mistakes
When He made them with care.
If love is a problem
For you to express,
Than give it to Jesus
And He'll do the rest.

Consuelo Cardenas

A Divided Home

We say we marry
Because we love.
But our mind and thoughts
Are far from love.
We look for love
In all the wrong places.
When we need to find God
To show us our places.
A house divided
Is no where to stay.
Because Jesus has
A better way.
He'll give you the strength
To never forget
That you're still His bride.
So don't be afraid
If he leaves you today.
Because Jesus will always
Be here to stay.

Precious Gift

We had it all
One time you see.
We had the car
And luxury.
We had a pool
To beat the heat.
While others had
No where to eat.
We ate and laughed
Our cares away.
Forgetting who had paid our way.
But know I have
A precious gift
It's Jesus Christ
Who gave me life.
The things I had
Were luxury.
Know all I want,
Is to be set free.

Consuelo Cardenas

Forgiveness

Sorrows come,
Sorrows go.
Sadness always take its tole.
But when you pray
And cry out to God.
He'll always say
Do not give up.
You may be hurt
Day after day.
But God will always whisper
To you and say,
"I love you child,
And don't forget.
I gave my Son,
So don't you quit.
He carried the cross
For you to see.
That all sins are forgiven
So let it be."

He Paid The Price

A price to pay
Will show you the way.
It doesn't come easy.
You'll find out one day.
A price to pay
Will show you which way.
It will give you direction
To the right way.
A price He paid,
It all happened one day.
He hung on a cross
And we're free today.
A price he paid
That we may have life.
So give it your all,
He did pay the price.

Consuelo Cardenas

A Laughing Matter

Laugh and laugh
And laugh more and more.
Your hurt will go
When you laugh some more.
It will heal you're hurt
I will heal your pain.
It's good medication
That will go through your veins.
So laugh
And laugh
And laugh again.
Don't let anyone
Keep you locked in.

Broken Vessel

God is the potter.
God uses his hands.
He'll shape you
And mold you
And give you a name.
He'll break you and build you
All over again.
So listen to Jesus,
Lest you break again.

Consuelo Cardenas

It's Nothing

A boat without foundation
Is nothing.
A building without a foundation
Is nothing.
A car without a motor
Is nothing.
A plane without wings,
Is nothing.
A church without a teacher
Is nothing
A tree without a fruit
Is nothing.
A body without a heart
Is nothing.
A person without love
Is nothing.
A person without God,
Is nothing.
All will perish
Without God.

Trusting the Lord

They come out from prison
All full of pride.
Trying to beat the system
When they hurt inside.
They carry themselves
Like there's no tomorrow.
Trying to solve a problem
With blows and horrors.
They pick up their face
And flex their muscles
Trying to scare people
With their grin.
And they smile,
But all it shows
Is how it could be
If he would only
Trust the Lord
To set him free.

Consuelo Cardenas

A Rooted Heart

Today is the day
That you said to me,
"Come here, my Child
You're going to be set free."
I struggled to say
All that I felt.
I had held it so long
It had rooted my hurt.
But then Jesus came
And fixed it up
And mended my heart
And made it all right.
He took every piece
That Satan had choked
And loosened those spirits
Of peace and of joy.
He gave me that boldness
That I need to say,
"I'm nobody's door mat.
Please love me this way.
The guilt that I carried
I've been forgiven.
Lets leave it that way."

Take Control

The mind can cause trouble.
The mind can cause pain.
The mind can tell stories
That will increase your pain.
The mind can be helpful.
It can change your whole life.
It's all up to you.
It's how you control your mind.

Consuelo Cardenas

Still Here

You say we left
Everything behind.
You started new,
You're doing fine.
But the things you say
You left behind
Were worldly goods;
They solved nothing.
You say you're here
To start again.
But you're mind is going;
The problem is still here.
Ask God for help.
Because you see
The things that you're carrying
Are still in thee.

Angels in Disguise

There came two angels
Knocking on my door.
One said, "How are you?"
The other said, "Hello."
They sat and asked
How was my day.
I started crying
I had too much to say.
They listened and listened
What I had to say.
They never said a word.
I had too much to say.
God sent them to me,
So I could be free.
And I tell everybody
Those angels healed me.

Consuelo Cardenas

Jesus Home

You sit at night alone
Wondering why
They left you behind.
You're getting old,
As you an see.
The kids are growing,
They want to be free.
But you must remember
We're not alone.
Jesus is with us.
We are his home.
He'll never leave us.
His word is true.
We should be happy,
His gift is you.

Forgive

Tomorrow's not promised.
The days are short.
Love your family
Because time is short.
There's no time for anger,
There's no time to spare.
So love your family
For tomorrow might
Not be there.
"Forgive and forget,"
God told me one day.
Love them no matter
How you feel any day.
Yesterday's gone.
Today's a new day.
Love your family
And bless them today.
A smile and a hug
Will brighten their day.
So let go of your anger
And start a new day.

Consuelo Cardenas

Love

Love is good.
Love is great.
Jesus comes
When we kneel and pray.
He'll heal our bodies
When we need it most,
And give us deliverance
And give us the Holy Ghost.
He'll teach us to fight
The enemy down
And give us authority
To tear strongholds down.
So listen my child,
And listen well.
Stay focused on Jesus
And you will prevail.

The Blood of Jesus

When the road gets tough
And you're ready to quit,
Remember who carried the cross
And got pierced
In his hands and his feet.
He carried the cross
For you and me.
And shed His blood
So we all could see.
That he did it,
So we could be free.

Consuelo Cardenas

Freedom to All

The crossroads of life
Will come into three.
You'll wonder why
It happened to thee.
The good that you do
Will show you the way,
Will bring freedom to all,
Who will follow your ways.
The crossroads of life
Will come unto thee.
They come with Jesus
So we can be free.

It's Never Easy

You had a man who hurt you,
Another man who died.
But because you loved your children.
You left all that behind.
Know you're going forward
It's not easy, as you can see.
But for God who's on your side
It's as easy as 1, 2, 3.
So focus on tomorrow
As new day's coming up.
You've already made it through this one.
God says, "Just don't give up."

Consuelo Cardenas

The Time is Near

Things come and things go.
We cherish things and then they go.
Our journey is short
And we don't know
What time or day
We may go.
Our Lord is near;
It is foretold.
So read and pray
And ask for strength
And God will do the rest.

A New Beginning

They come and go,
On these streets of fate.
They have no direction
They have no one who waits.
They're hungry.
They're tired,
No place to rest.
Their days filled
With hustling and begging
They're mothers and fathers
Who once had it all.
But for some reason,
They lost everything.
But there is life,
If you give it to God.
And let God to the rest.

Consuelo Cardenas

Be Thankful

Thank you, Lord,
For loving me.
Thank you, Lord,
For correcting me.
Thank you, Lord,
For Jesus
Thank you, Lord,
For our ups and downs
Thank you, Lord,
For our good over our bad.
Thank you, Lord,
For our trials and tribulations.
Thank you, Lord,
For our children.
Thank you, Lord,
For my spouse.
Thank you, Lord,
For our jobs.
Thank you, Lord,
For our home.
Thank you, Lord,
For our car.
Thank you, Lord,
For the cross.

Stay Focused

Remember this;
Remember it well.
The Devil torments
If you're not in prayer.
He'll prowl around
Like a lion at night,
And attack you when
All things seem all right.
He targets you're mind
And gets you confused.
And plants everything
That is not good for you.
So stay in prayer
And focus on God.
Because God is our light
And he'll make things all right.

Consuelo Cardenas

It Takes Two

It takes two
To raise a child.
It takes two
To set them straight.
It takes two
To pray together.
So that child
Will not be afraid.
It takes two
So stay together,
Even when it's tough for you.
So love your child
Whole heartedly
And all your prayer
Will come through.

Seasons Come and Go

Precious is the season
That comes through every year.
The leaves that grow in spring
Tell summer's almost here.
Precious are the hours
That we spend in prayer.
Because just like the seasons,
We know our time is near.
So pray on all occasions
No matter how you feel.
Because just as seasons come and go
Jesus will soon be here.

Consuelo Cardenas

Fear, the Unknown

Fear is not Love.
Fear is not happiness.
Fear cripples a soul
And makes you helpless.
Fear can help you;
It warns you all day.
To be alert
And not go that way.
So if you fear
The unknown,
Pray for guidance.
God won't leave you alone.

Blessed Prayer

The prayers I pray
Will always be
A blessing for you and me.
No matter what
The day will bring,
The prayers I pray
Will set you free.
So don't give up,
And pray for me,
So God can use us
To set others free.

Consuelo Cardenas

Grandmas

Grandmas are here
Every day of the year.
To love and cherish
Every one that comes near.
They sit and they stare
Wanting to say,
I know that you're hurting
So let's start to pray.
Her eyes look so tired.
Her body's so frail.
But she listens to others
As they pour out themselves.
She loves them and hugs them
And loves them some more.
Know that her days
Might not be many more.
She sits on her rocker,
Wanting to see
How many grandchildren
Want to be set free.
So go see your grandma
And take her advice.
She's a woman of wisdom
And she loves Jesus Christ.

Bring it Out

We waste our time
Wondering why
Our precious life
Has gone so dry.
We say this,
We say that.
We eat this,
And drink that,
And blame everyone.
And its not even that.
We fail to see
It's deep inside.
You need to bring it
Back outside.
Let God show you
How to be true
So you're precious life
Can shine all night through.

Consuelo Cardenas

Love Yourself

Love yourself,
If you want healing.
Love yourself
If you want love.
Love yourself
So you can love others.
Love yourself
And you'll love everyone.

Answered Prayer

I look for answers in the night
When lights are low
And moon is bright.
I search my heart
And all I feel
Is a wounded spirit that cannot be healed.
I turn to God
So he can see
The pain that's going through all of me.
If I could hear
Your voice tonight
I'll know I'll make it through this night.
So bring me, Lord,
Some dreams tonight
And speak to me
So I can see
The promise that you made to me.

www.ingramcontent.com/pod-product-compliance
Lightning Source LLC
Chambersburg PA
CBHW050602300426
44112CB00013B/2030